D1245320

WHAT'S THE CRAIC?

The Hilarious Pocket Guide to Irish Slang

Brian Doyle

Table of Contents

Chapter One

The Mighty Craic-Filled Guide to Irish Slang

INTRODUCTION

"Irish slang is like a secret code - it's full of hidden meanings and nuances that only the Irish can truly understand. It's a part of our culture, and it's something that connects us to our roots."

Dara Ó Brian, Irish Comedian

"Ireland is a place of great beauty and history, but it's also a place of great warmth and hospitality. It's a place where you can feel at home no matter where you come from."

Pierce Brosnan, Irish Actor

We bid you a hearty welcome to the country of leprechauns, shamrocks, and Guinness, where language finds an entirely new dimension of humor and charm. If you're up for some craic and want to sound like an authentic native Irish speaker, then fasten your seatbelt and get ready to immerse yourself in the land of Irish slang!

Irish slang is a gas craic of expressions and idioms that reflect the country's deep cultural heritage as well as its renowned sense of humor. Every term, from the snarky "**gee-eyed**" to the baffling "**banjaxed**" is like a pot of gold just waiting to be discovered.

But don't be fooled into thinking it's all grand and dandy; Irish slang can be a fierce beast to catch on to, since so many regions and dialects have their own distinct takes on similar terms. In Dublin, for instance, a "**shift**" refers to a snog; in Cork, on the other hand, it is a "**ride**" that will do the job.

Yet, you shouldn't 'act the maggot' because we're here to serve as your reliable tour guide on the path to being a true connoisseur in Irish slang. We'll guide you through the correct usage of these expressions and ensure you have a good laugh along the way.

Whether you're planning a trip to the Emerald Isle or simply want to add some Irish charm to your vocabulary, this guide to Irish slang will have you sounding like a local in no time. So, sit down , grab a pint of the black stuff, and let's explore the wonderful world of Irish slang together!

Chapter Two

"What's the Craic?"

IRISH GREETINGS

"When you're greeted with an Irish slang phrase like 'What's the craic?', you know you're in for a good time. It's the perfect invitation to let your hair down."

Graham Norton, Irish Comedian

"As a musician who has spent a lot of time in Ireland, I've come to appreciate the unique and friendly nature of Irish slang greetings. Hearing 'How's she cutting?' always puts me in a good mood."

Ed Sheeran, English Singer-Songwriter

W ell then, we should start with some introductions, shouldn't we? Greetings in Ireland often begin with "**What's the craic?**" as you might have guessed. But don't worry, it doesn't mean what you might think at first...

It's actually a casual method of inquiring about someone's wellbeing and whether or not anything exciting has happened in their life lately. It's all a part of the great Irish banter.

But don't fret, there's plenty of alternative choices too. In Dublin, locals might ask, "**What's the story?**" or "**What's the craic?**". Meanwhile, in Cork, "**How's she cutting?**" or "**How are you keeping?**" are more common choices.

So, now that you've got the conversation going, how do you continue? Well, don't be shy about throwing some comedy and wit into your conversations; the Irish are masters of both. Rather than responding with a simple "good" or "fine," try something more interesting the next time someone asks how you are doing. Some examples of acceptable responses include "I haven't won the lotto just yet" and "pure hanging but grand altogether, thanks for asking."

But remember, some certain expressions are best to be avoided if you aren't true Irish. Avoid using the charming-sounding but really unheard-of-in-Ireland "**Top of the morning to ya**" unless you want your newfound Irish friend to bolt from you like an escaped gazelle. Likewise, the phrase "**Kiss me, I'm Irish**" is another cringeworthy St. Patrick's Day cliché that the Irish despise.

The Irish custom of asking, "**Story?**" as a kind greeting is widespread across the country. The question is a condensed form of "**What's the story?**" and is used to inquire into someone's well-being or the recent events in their lives.

What's the story, morning glory? - In Ireland, this is a common way to greet someone in a fun or flirtatious manner.

Story, horse? (STOR-ee hors) – Another alternative to "What's the craic?" is an Irish expression that's short for "what's the story?" A more casual type of greeting, this one is often reserved for use amongst close friends or acquaintances. If you happen to meet into a friend on the street, you can ask, "Story horse? A "story horse" is also a person who is continuously making things up.

What's the craic? (pronounced "krak") – So what actually is the craic? The Irish term for fun or good times is craic. What someone truly means when they ask, "What's the craic?" is either "What's the fun?" or "What's going on?" Among Irish people of all ages, but notably the younger generation, this is a common way to say hello.

Any craic? (anny krak) - What's the craic is a slang term for "what's going on" or "what's the deal." This informal greeting is common among friends and those who are otherwise familiar with one another. "Any craic?" is a phrase commonly used when friends get together for a drink.

What's crackin'? (whats CRACK-in) - This is a colloquial way of saying "What's up?" or "What's up with you?" When speaking casually between friends or acquaintances, this is the language of choice. During a party, you may ask someone, "What's cracking?" to strike up a conversation.

Hows she cuttin? (hows shee KUHT-in) - Meaning "How are you doing?" or "What's up?", this is a casual form of greeting. It's common in more relaxed circumstances amongst friends and acquaintances. The phrase "Hey, how's she cutting?" is a common greeting amongst bar friends.

Grand - When an Irish person says they are "grand" it is taken as a given that they are satisfied and happy with life. It may be used to convey a variety of emotions, including pleasure, contentment, and happiness.

It's also a typical way of saying something is not a big deal or to play down a serious situation. "How are you?" "I'm grand."

I'M GRAND.

Grand so - When asked a question or made a request, this is a typical Irish answer. Meaning "okay" or "that's alright," it's used to signal agreement or approval.

Grand stretch - The informal Irish greeting "grand stretch" is commonly used among friends. It's used to acknowledge someone's presence or to let someone know everything is well.

Howya - (HOY-ya) - A traditional Irish greeting that means "how are you?" It's a common way to say hello to those you know, and the typical answer is "great" or "not too terrible."

What about ye? (what a-bout ye?) - This colloquial hello is common in rural areas, so be prepared to hear it. A simple way of asking "how are things?" upon running across an old friend or acquaintance.

Hiya (HI-yuh) - The phrase "hello there" has been reduced to "hiya" over the years. It's a kind, casual greeting typically exchanged among people already familiar with one another. When you run into a friend on the street, you could greet them with a "Hiya," for instance.

Top of the morning (top ov the morn-in) - This is a traditional Irish greeting that is typically linked to St. Patrick's Day and leprechauns. In other words, it's a nice way to offer your best wishes for someone's day. As already mentioned, it's best to avoid this one unless you're looking to start a brawl (a fight).

Fair play - In Ireland, this is a common expression of praise. It's a universal method of showing appreciation for someone else's efforts or acts of kindness. One can say "fair play to you" to someone who has just finished a challenging assignment or done something remarkable.

How's the form? This is a slang way of saying "how are you feeling physically?" after a night of heavy drinking or partying. You can expect a "hanging" or "dying" response from a hungover individual.

Dia dhuit (dee-a gwit) - This traditional Irish greeting translates to "God be with you" in English. The standard response is "Dia is Muire dhuit," and it is reserved for more formal occasions (God and Mary be with you).

How're you keeping? (hou-er yew kee-pin) - Often used as a greeting in Ireland, it's another Irish equivalent of "how are you?"

Well boy – Mostly used among young Irish lads, this is a friendly way to say "hi" or "what's up?" to someone you just met. You may ask a friend you run into on the street, "Well boy, how's it going?" as an example.

How's the head? (hows the HED) - After a few drinks, this is a standard Irish greeting. The question, which is a euphemism for "How's your head feeling? ", is commonly used to ascertain whether or not the respondent is suffering from a hangover. When you see a buddy the day after a party, you can ask, "How's the head?" to find out if they're feeling okay.

When you haven't seen someone for a long time, you might say "**Long time no see**" (LONG tyme noh see). This gesture symbolizes the passage of time since you two were last together. You could use the phrase "Long time no see" when you see a buddy after a long absence, say, a few months.

Slán (SLAWN) - Often used as a kind of farewell in Ireland, this phrase originates from Irish. It can be used formally or informally and signifies "safe" or "sound" in its original context. You might tell someone you're leaving that "Slán go fóill" (goodbye for now).

Chapter Three

"This beer is very sessionable."

A DEADLY SESH

"The Irish love their craic - it's like crack, but with more laughs and fewer side effects."

Ed Byrne, Irish Actor

T he Irish are known for being the life of a party, and knowing just a wee bit of the local lingo will help you feel right at home. First, you must learn the traditional Irish toast "**Sláinte!**" which literally means "health." Raise a pint glass and toast your new Irish pals with a hearty "sláinte!" to prove you've got what it takes to hang with them at the local watering hole.

When everyone in the bar is seated, the term "**jammers**" is used to describe the situation – packed to the brim. If you want to have a drink at the bar, you might have to shove your way in, but the craic is totally worth it.

Attending a "**session**" or "**trad sesh**" guarantees a good time. Taking in some traditional Irish tunes during a session is a terrific opportunity to get a feel for the local culture. The convenience of a friend's home as a meeting place allows for a more casual session. It's nothing more than a bunch of folks coming together to have a good time with some booze and good banter. It's common to use the terms "**bevvies**" and "**scoops**" when referring to a trip to the pub for a few beers. But don't stay up all night "**quaffing**" beer and find yourself in need of a "fag break" to recover.

Lastly, a "**beor**" is a female, so keep that in mind if you hear the word. It's a cute way of saying she enjoys having fun and making others laugh. Thus, if you happen to run across a beor at the local watering hole, treat her to a beverage and join in the conversation.

Sláinte! (slawn-cha) - As we mentioned, this is a standard Irish cheers. Let's drink to our health, therefore let's raise a glass and say, "sláinte!" The term has its origins in the Irish language, and is widely used at parties and other festive occasions all over the world. This is a gesture meant to convey good health and happiness to others around you.

Gaff party (gaf par-tee) - "This weekend, I'm hosting a gaff party at my place." A gaff party, otherwise known as a "house party," is a social gathering that takes place in a private residence rather than a public place like a bar or club. It is a frequent Irish phrase for a small, social gathering of close friends.

Quaffing (kwaff-ing) is slang for downing enormous quantities of alcohol in a short amount of time. " It was a night full of beer pong and quaffing pints."

Banter (ban-ter) - A lighthearted way of joking around with friends in a teasing and playful way. "We had some great banter."

Beor (bay-ore) - Often, this is a compliment directed at a woman. "She's a fantastic beor, always up for a good laugh."

Jammers - (jam-ers) This slang term means a place or situation is extremely crowded or full. For example, "The pub was jammers last night, we could barely move!" The word is likely derived from the word "jam," meaning to pack or fill tightly. Jammers is often used to describe a situation where there are too many people in one place, making it difficult to move or breathe. The term can be used in a negative or positive sense, depending on the context.

Deadly - (ded-lee) This means something is cool or excellent. For example, "That concert was deadly, I had so much fun!" The word has its roots in the Irish language, where "ólta" meant fatal or deadly. Over time, it evolved to mean something was exciting or enjoyable. Deadly is a common slang term in Ireland and is often used to describe something that is especially impressive or exciting.

Bevvies - (bev-ees) "We're going out for a few bevvies tonight." Bevvies is a slang term for drinks or alcoholic beverages. It is a popular term in Ireland and is often used when friends are planning to go out and have a few drinks together.

Sesh - (sesh) "We're having a sesh at my friend's house tonight." Sesh is a slang term for a gathering of people to drink and socialize, often used by young people. It is a common term in Ireland and is often used to describe a small, informal gathering of friends.

Crackin' - (crack-in) "The pub was crackin' last night." Crackin' is a term for a lively and energetic atmosphere, often used in the context of social events. It is a popular term in Ireland and is often used to describe a night out with friends or a lively party atmosphere.

Sessionable - (session-able) "This beer is very sessionable." Sessionable is a term for a beer that is easy to drink in large quantities without getting too drunk. It is a popular term in Ireland and is often used to describe beers that have a lower alcohol content and are designed for socializing and drinking over a longer period of time.

Rasher - (rah-sher) This is a term used to describe a good-looking person, usually in a playful or flirtatious way. For example, "Did you see the rasher at the bar last night? I couldn't take my eyes off her."

Fag break - (fag break) This is a term used to describe a break from partying or drinking to go outside and smoke a cigarette. "I'm going to take a quick fag break, I'll be back in a few minutes." The term is used in Ireland and other parts of the world where smoking is common.

Coddin ya - (cod-din yah) This means to tease or joke with someone. It is a common term in Ireland and is often used when friends are joking around with each other. For example, "Are you serious or are you just coddin ya?"

Pure craic - (pyoor crack) As we already mentioned, craic is an Irish term for fun or good times. Adding "pure" emphasizes that something is particularly enjoyable or entertaining. For example, "Last night was pure craic, we had such a great time."

Scuttered - (skut-erd) This term is used to describe someone who is very drunk. For example, "He was scuttered after only a few drinks, we had to help him get home."

The jacks - (the jax) This is a slang term for the bathroom or toilet. For example, "Excuse me, can you tell me where the jacks are?"

Shook - (shook) This term is used to describe someone who is visibly upset or scared. For example, "She was so shook after watching that horror movie, she couldn't sleep all night."

Hallion - (Hal-leon) This playful term describes someone who is a bit naughty. Example: "He's some Hallion, that lad!"

Quare - (kw-air) This is often used to emphasise that something is really great. Example: "It's quare weather today!"

The '10 Commandments' of Irish Pub Shenanigans

The Irish pub… a cultural institution rich in tradition, history, and, of course, copious pints of the black stuff. But, for those who haven't had the pleasure of experiencing the warmth and camaraderie of a true Irish pub, there are some unwritten rules of etiquette to remember. Here are the ten holy commandments for how to conduct yourself in an Irish pub:

1. **Never order a half-pint**: Nothing says "tourist" like ordering a half-pint in an Irish pub. If you can't handle a full pint, try a glass of water instead or go home and watch Netflix.

2. **Thou shalt not mention leprechauns**: We get it, you think making a leprechaun joke is cute. But believe us when we say it's not funny. It's actually quite irritating.

3. **Thou shalt not sit in someone else's favorite spot at the bar**: Every Irish pub has its regulars, and they all have their favorite spots at the bar. Don't take someone else's seat if you don't want to risk being ejected.

4. **Thou shalt not drink alone**: The entire purpose of an Irish pub is to socialize and meet new people. If you're going to sit alone, you might as well stay at home.

5. **Do not order a drink with ice**: We prefer our

drinks at room temperature in Ireland. So, before you order a whiskey, make sure you know what you're getting yourself into.

6. **Thou shalt not bemoan the music**: If you don't like the traditional Irish music playing in the background, that's your problem. The pub's music will not change just because you don't appreciate the beauty of the bodhrán.

7. **Do not talk on your phone loudly**: No one wants to hear your conversation about your cousin's wedding while they're trying to enjoy their Guinness. Put your phone on silent and limit your conversations.

8. **Do not order a drink and then leave**: Irish pubs are all about taking your time and savoring your drink. You might as well have stayed at home if you're going to order a drink and then dash out the door.

9. **Do not forget to tip**: Tipping is a way of showing appreciation for good service in Ireland. Make sure to leave a few coins on the bar if you want to make friends with the bartender.

10. **Thou shalt not depart without saying farewell**: Irish farewells are notorious for being lengthy and drawn-out affairs. Don't leave without saying goodbye to your new friends. Who knows, maybe you'll get a free drink out of it.

Chapter Four

"It'll be Grand"

EXPRESSING EMOTION

"Being Irish, he had an abiding sense of tragedy, which sustained him through temporary periods of joy."

William Butler Yeats

The Irish are known for their passion, but they are not always comfortable expressing their feelings openly. While they may not whoop and holler or cry easily in public, they do have a softer side that comes out in more subtle ways behind closed doors.

Imagine someone saying, **"Ah, sure it'll be grand"** in response to a difficult situation. This seemingly simple phrase is dense with meaning; it implies that everything will work out in the end and that there is no point in worrying about things over which you have no control. It reflects the Irish spirit in some ways: optimistic, resilient, and always looking on the bright side of things.

"**The craic**" is another expression that captures the Irish way of life. This phrase refers to the good times, laughter, and fun that come from being in good company. The craic is taken seriously in Ireland; it is more than just drinking and telling jokes; it is about connecting with others and celebrating life's joys.

While the Irish do not wear their hearts on their sleeves, they do have a rich and nuanced way of expressing their emotions. You'll be able to appreciate the depth of feeling that lies beneath the surface if you know a little Irish slang.

BILL WAS EVEN MORE IMPRESSED BY THEIR ENERGY AND ALCOHOL TOLERANCE WHEN HE FOUND OUT THAT CRAIC DIDN'T MEAN WHAT HE THOUGHT IT DID.

Delighted – (dih-LAHY-tid) If you're not delighted with this definition, sure you must be a sourpuss. Delighted means to be very happy or pleased with something. It's the feeling you get when you find a fiver on the street, when your team wins the match, or when someone buys you a pint unexpectedly. Example: "I'm absolutely delighted to hear you got the job. Well done!"

Banjaxed – (BAN-jakst) Ah, the classic Irish way of describing anything that's broken or destroyed. Can also mean very tired or exhausted, as if you've been up all night with the Banshee. If something is banjaxed, you can either try to fix it with a bit of spit and polish, or you can just give up and have a pint instead. Example: "The car is banjaxed, so we'll have to take the bus to the match tonight."

Fecked – (fekd) This one has a few meanings, depending on the context. It can mean tired, exhausted, or ruined. It's also a versatile exclamation of surprise or disbelief, perfect for when you find out your mate's won the lotto or when you hear that the match has been cancelled due to rain. Example: "I'm absolutely fecked after that run, I need to sit down."

Gobsmacked – (gob-smakt) When you're gobsmacked, you're surprised or stunned, often used in response to unexpected news or events. It's the feeling you get when your team wins the All-Ireland, or when you find out that the price of Guinness has gone down. Example: "I was absolutely gobsmacked when he told me he was getting married."

Langered – (LAN-jerd) When you're langered, you're drunk, often to the point of seeing leprechauns. It's the feeling you get when you've had a few too many pints of the black stuff or when you've been playing a drinking game with your mates. Example: "We got absolutely langered last night, I don't even remember getting home."

Bollixed – (BOL-ikst) If you're bollixed, you're confused or mixed up. It can also mean in trouble or screwed over. It's the Irish way of describing a situation that's gone pear-shaped or a person who's made a mess of things. Example: "I'm completely bollixed with this math problem, I can't make sense of it."

Wagon – (Y-gon) is a phrase used to refer to a woman who is difficult to deal with or unpleasant in nature. Example: "God, she's such a wagon at work!"

Pissed off – (pist awf) When you're pissed off, you're angry or annoyed, usually in response to something someone has done. It's the feeling you get when someone cuts in front of you in the queue at the chipper or when your boss gives you more work to do on a Friday afternoon. Example: "I was so pissed off when he cancelled our plans at the last minute."

Sound – (saund) If someone is sound, they're a solid, dependable, and trustworthy individual. It's the Irish way of complimenting someone's character, expressing that they are a decent human being who can be relied upon. If a friend does you a favor, you might say "thanks, you're sound out".

Gas - (gass) Gas means funny or hilarious, and is often used to describe a joke or situation that made you laugh out loud. It's a term that's particularly popular in Dublin and other urban areas. Example: "Did you hear that story? It was gas, I couldn't stop laughing. John's such a funny guy, he always knows how to make us laugh.

Up the walls – (up thuh wawls) When you're up the walls, you're feeling overwhelmed or stressed out. It can also mean being very busy or occupied. This phrase is often used to describe the feeling of having too much to do and not enough time to do it. If you're up the walls, you might need a cuppa tea and a sit down to relax.

Pure – (pyoor) In Ireland, this word is frequently used to emphasize the degree or intensity of something, such as being "pure knackered" or "pure starving". It's a way of expressing extreme exhaustion or hunger. You might use it to describe how tired you are after a long day at work or how hungry you feel after skipping breakfast.

Feckin' eejit – (FEK-in AY-jit) This phrase is often used playfully to tease someone who is acting silly or foolish. It's a lighthearted insult that's usually used among friends. If your friend accidentally spills their pint at the pub, you might jokingly call them a feckin' eejit.

Bollocks – (BOL-iks) This word can have various meanings, but when used to describe someone's emotions or feelings, it usually means they're frustrated, annoyed, or angry about something. It's a forceful word that's more expressive than simply saying "annoyed" or "irritated". You might use it to describe your feelings towards your boss after they cancel your vacation plans.

Pissed – (pist) In Ireland, this term is often used to mean drunk or intoxicated, but it can also be used to describe someone who is very angry or annoyed about something. It's a versatile word that can convey both positive and negative emotions. If your friend is acting rowdy after a few pints, you might say they're pissed.

Shtuck – (shtuhk) This word is used to describe a feeling of being stuck or trapped in a frustrating or difficult situation. It conveys a sense of helplessness or hopelessness, as if there's no way out of the problem. You might use it to describe your feelings when you're stuck in a traffic jam on the way to an important appointment.

Happy out - (hap-ee owt) Happy out is a slang term used to describe someone who is happy and content with their life. It is often used as a response to a question about someone's well-being. Example: "How are you doing these days?" "Oh, I'm happy out, thanks for asking."

Begrudger - (buh-gruj-er) Begrudger is a slang term used to describe someone who is jealous or envious of someone else's success. It is often used to criticize someone who is not happy for others. Example: "Don't listen to him, he's just a begrudger. He can't stand it when other people do well."

YOU HAVE TO BE
BOLD AS BRASS
TO DEAL WITH BULLIES!

Bold - (bowl-d) Bold is a slang term used to describe someone who is mischievous or rebellious. It is often used to describe children who are behaving badly. Example: "My son was so bold at school today, he got into a fight with another kid."

Feisty - (fay-stee) Feisty is a slang term used to describe someone who is spirited or full of energy. It can be used to describe someone who is argumentative or someone who is full of life. Example: "She's always been feisty, she never backs down from an argument."

Scundered - (Skun-derd) A common slang term used for when you feel embarrassed or fed up with something. Example: "work had me pure scundered!"

Chapter Five

"Pint of the Black Stuff, Please!"

PUB TALK

"Food is our common ground, a universal experience."

James Beard

For many Irish people, going to the pub is more than just a place to grab a drink; it's a cultural institution. With peat fires crackling, friendly locals chatting, and traditional music filling the air, the typical Irish bar exudes warmth and hospitality.

But the language used in Irish pubs is also distinctive. When you're "**on the lash**", you're in the process of becoming inebriated. If you're "**off your trolley**", you're completely out of control. And if you've had a few too many drinks, you might declare yourself "**totally langered**".

However, the pub is more than just a drinking den; it's also a place for lively conversation, storytelling, and making new friends. And what better way to toast good company than with a hearty "**Sláinte!**" (meaning "to your health")?

So, whether you're a local or a visitor, don't miss out on the great craic at your nearby Irish pub. With its convivial atmosphere and welcoming regulars, it's the perfect spot to unwind and have some fun. Just make sure not to go overboard and end up looking like a stuffed Catholic school on Pancake Tuesday!

Guinness - (gihn-ness) A dark Irish stout that is famous all over the world. It's a beloved symbol of Irish culture and is enjoyed by many as a rich and creamy beer. Example: "Let's head down to the pub and grab a pint of Guinness."

Whiskey - (wiss-key) A type of alcoholic beverage made from fermented grain mash, typically aged in oak barrels. Irish whiskey is known for its smooth and mellow taste. Example: "After a long day, there's nothing better than a glass of Irish whiskey to unwind."

Fancy a jar? - (fahn-see uh jar) A common Irish expression that means "Do you want to go to the pub and have some drinks with me?" Example: "Hey, fancy a jar after work?"

Banger - (bang-ur) A term used to describe a sausage, especially a breakfast sausage. Example: "I could really go for some bangers and mash right now." The term can also refer to a really good song such as "that song is a banger!"

Local - (loh-kull) A slang term for a pub or bar that is frequented by locals. Example: "Let's head down to the local and grab a pint."

Lad - (lahd) A term used to refer to a friend, mate or buddy. Example: "Alright, lad. How's it going?"

Your shout - (yor sh-owt) A phrase used to indicate that it's someone's turn to buy a round of drinks for the group. Example: "Thanks for the pint, mate. My shout next time."

It has great scran though... - (it has grayt skran thoh) A phrase used to indicate that although the establishment or situation may not be ideal, the food is good. Example: "The pub might be a bit run down, but it has great scran though."

Ride, shift, shiftin', shiftin' stones - (ryd, shif, shif-tin, shif-tin stoh-ns) All terms used to refer to trying to flirt with someone or ask them out, usually in a clumsy or inappropriate way. Example: "Don't be that guy who's always shiftin' stones in the pub. It's not a good look."

Get one in - (get wun in) A phrase used to ask someone to buy a round of drinks for the group. Example: "I'm heading to the bar. Anyone want me to get one in?"

On the pull - (on the pul) A phrase used to describe someone who is actively seeking a sexual partner, usually in a bar or nightclub setting. Example: "He's been on the pull all night. I don't think he'll have much luck."

Naggin – (Nag-in) This term refers to a small bottle of alcohol, usually 200ml. Example: "Can I get a naggin of vodka?"

Upchuck - (up-chuhk) A slang term used to describe vomiting or throwing up, usually after drinking too much. Example: "I had too much to drink last night and ended up upchucking in the bathroom."

See a man about a horse - (see uh man uh-bout uh hors) A euphemism for going to the bathroom, often used to avoid directly stating it in polite company. Example: "Excuse me, I need to see a man about a horse."

Time, gentlemen, please! - (tahym, jen-tuhl-muhn, pleez) A phrase used to signal the end of drinking time at a pub or bar, often accompanied by the ringing of a bell. Example: "Time, gentlemen, please! Last call for drinks."

Scoops - (skoops) Another term for alcoholic drinks, particularly beer or lager. Example: "I'm going to the bar to get some more scoops, do you want anything?"

Locked - (lahkt) A term used to describe being very drunk or intoxicated. Example: "I can't remember anything from last night. I was absolutely locked."

Pint of plain - This is a common way to order a pint of Guinness in Ireland. It's a reference to the simple and classic nature of the beer, which is a staple in Irish pubs.

I'M OFF MY TROLLY!
J

Off my trolley- (off me trolley) This playful phrase refers to someone who was really drunk the night before. Example: "I was off my trolley last night lad!"

Snug – (Snug) This is a small, private room in a pub where groups of friends can gather for a pint and some conversation away from the main bar area. It's often cozy and intimate, with comfortable seating and low lighting. Example: "Let's head to the snug for a quieter drink and catch up."

Lock-in - (lahk-in) This is a secret gathering that takes place in a pub after closing time, when the doors are locked and the drinks continue to flow. It's illegal but can be a fun and memorable experience for those who are lucky enough to be invited. Example: "We had a mad lock-in at the pub last night, we didn't leave until sunrise!"

Irish Pub Characters: The Good, the Bad, and the Drunk

The Irish pub is a cultural institution that has brought people together for centuries. But what about the people you'll meet? Don't worry, my friend, because I'm here to walk you through the various types of characters you'll encounter in your local pub.

First up are the **"craic pack."** These are the people who are always aware of where the party is taking place. They'll be the ones at the bar, giggling and joking with everyone. They're up for anything, whether it's a game of cards, a sing-song, or some good old-fashioned banter. These people are the life of the party and will ensure that you have a good time as well. Just be careful not to get too caught up in the fun, or you might wake up with a headache the next day!

There are also **"local characters."** These are the pub regulars who know everyone. They're the people who have been coming here for years and have stories to tell. They'll be at the bar, holding court and entertaining everyone with stories from their youth. They'll have odd habits and sayings, but they'll always make you laugh. Just don't try to take their seat at the bar or you'll be met with a death stare.

The **"lager louts"** are up next. They're the ones who can't stop drinking and aren't afraid to start a fight. They'll be the ones at the back of the bar, yelling at each other and downing pints like they're going out of style. Avoid, unless you want to get into trouble.

There are also the **"quiet ones."** These are the people who sit in the corner with a pint in their hand, watching the world go by. They're not looking for a good time or company; they just want to have a quiet drink in peace. They may appear aloof at first, but if you strike up a conversation with them, you'll discover that they, too, have some interesting stories to tell.

Let us not forget about the **"tourists."** These are the people who have traveled long distances to experience the magic of an Irish pub. They'll be the ones taking pictures of everything, attempting to learn some Irish phrases, and generally appearing to be having a good time. They may not be familiar with all of the local customs and traditions, but they are eager to learn and have fun.

Of course, these are only a few of the characters you might encounter in an Irish pub. There are also "musicians" who come in for a jam session, **"young ones"** who are out for a night on the town, and "old timers" who remember when the pub was the center of the community. But regardless of who you meet, one thing is certain: you're in for a good time. So grab a pint, a stool, and join in on the fun.

Sláinte!

Chapter Six

"We're at Bridget's New Gaff, Come!"

IN ME GAFF

"May your home always be too small to hold all your friends."

Traditional Irish Blessing

In Ireland, the concept of "home" extends beyond a physical location. It's a gathering place for family and friends to share stories, laughs, and good times. It's a sacred place where you can be completely yourself, kick up your heels, and let your hair down.

Irish people are very proud of their homes, whether they are cozy cottages in the countryside or bustling city flats. Many people regard their home as a reflection of their identity and personality, and they pour their hearts and souls into making it a welcoming and comfortable space.

But it's not just the physical space that influences how the Irish view their humble abodes; it's also the culture of craic and hospitality. Hospitality is a way of life in Ireland, and visitors are always welcomed into homes with open arms.

That is why, when discussing homes in Ireland, it is critical to have a few key phrases and slang terms in your back pocket. You might hear someone refer to their house as a **"gaff"** or their bedroom as a **"kip."** And if you're invited to someone's home for a party or gathering, you can count on a warm welcome and plenty of fun.

Indeed, some of the best memories are created in the warmth of an Irish home, surrounded by family and friends. There's always something going on in an Irish household, from Sunday dinners to lively game nights.

So, the next time you visit Ireland, take some time to appreciate the country's unique hospitality culture and the value of home. And if you're fortunate enough to be invited into someone's home, bring your best self and get ready for a night of craic, laughter, and unforgettable memories.

Pad - (pad) Another term for a house or apartment, often used in casual conversation. For example, "I'm just chilling in my pad." The term comes from the idea of a place where one can rest their feet, or "pad" around.

Crash pad - (krash pad) This is a term used to describe a place where someone can crash or stay for a short period of time. For example, "I'm staying in a friend's crash pad for the weekend." The term comes from the idea of a place where one can rest or "crash" for a bit.

Diggs - (digs) This term is used to describe someone's living quarters. For example, "I'm heading back to my diggs." The term comes from the verb "to dig," which means to burrow or settle in, reflecting the sense of comfort one feels in their own space.

Gaff - (gaf) This is a popular Irish slang term used to describe a house or apartment. For example, "I'm heading back to the gaff now." The origin of the term is uncertain, but it's believed to have originated in the Dublin area.

Bleedin' hovel - (blee-din huv-el) This term is used to describe a dirty or run-down place. For example, "I can't believe you're living in that bleedin' hovel!" The term comes from the word "hovel," which means a small, dirty dwelling.

Doss house - (doss hows) This term is used to describe a cheap, dirty, and rundown hostel or hotel. For example, "I stayed in a doss house when I was traveling on a tight budget." The term comes from the slang term "doss," meaning to sleep or rest, reflecting the idea of a place to crash for a night.

I'M OUT OF WORK AT THE MOMENT SO IT'S JUST DIGS N' SAWDUST FOR NOW!

Digs n' sawdust – (DIGZ n' SAW-duhst) This term is used to describe a cheap and basic accommodation, often found in rural areas. For example, "We stayed in some digs n' sawdust while we were hiking in the countryside." The term comes from the idea of a basic, rough-and-ready place to stay, often with sawdust on the floor.

Fleapit - (flē-pit) This term is used to describe a rundown or shabby cinema or theatre. For example, "I went to see a movie in a fleapit last night, the seats were so uncomfortable!" The term comes from the idea of a flea-infested place, where one would not want to stay for long.

Kip - (kip) This term is used to describe a dirty or messy place. For example, "I can't believe how much of a kip this room is!" The term comes from the idea of a place where one can sleep, but not comfortably, reflecting a sense of disarray or chaos.

Gombeen house - (gum-been hows) This term is used to describe a house that is overcrowded or poorly maintained. For example, "I can't stand going to his gombeen house, it's always so cramped and messy." The term comes from the Irish word "gombeen," which refers to a person who profits from small-scale transactions, often used to describe someone who takes advantage of others.

Bolt-hole - (bolt-hohl) This term is used to describe a small, secluded place where someone can escape from the world. For example, "I'm heading to my bolt-hole in the countryside to get away from the city for a while." The term comes from the idea of a place where one can bolt or lock oneself away, a secret hideaway.

Jackeen mansion – (JACK-een MAN-shun) This term is used to describe a small, cramped, or poorly designed house or apartment. For example, "I can't believe they're charging so much for this jackeen mansion!" The term comes from the word "jackeen," which was historically used as a derogatory term for someone from Dublin.

Gombeen landlord – (GUM-been LAN-dlord) This term is used to describe a landlord who is greedy, exploitative, or neglectful. For example, "Our gombeen landlord never fixes anything, even when we tell him about it." The term comes from the Irish word "gombeen," which refers to a person who profits from small-scale transactions.

Cat's kitchen – (CATS KITCH-en) This term is used to describe a small, cluttered, or poorly organized kitchen. For example, "I can barely fit all my dishes in this cat's kitchen!" The term comes from the idea of a kitchen that is so small or disorganized that it's only suitable for a cat.

Bleedin' shoebox – (BLEED-in SHOO-box) This term is used to describe a very small or cramped living space, such as a studio apartment or small bedroom. For example, "I can't believe how much rent they're charging for this bleedin' shoebox!" The term comes from the idea of a space that is so small, it's only suitable for storing shoes.

Grá den phlás – (GRAW den FLOSS) This term is used to describe a love of luxury or opulence, often at the expense of practicality or common sense. For example, "She spent all her savings on that fancy car, she has a real grá den phlás." The term comes from the Irish phrase "grá den phlás," which means "love of display."

Burrow – (BUHR-o) This term is used to describe a small, cozy living space. For example, "I love my little burrow, it's perfect for me." The term comes from the idea of a burrow or underground dwelling.

The North-South Divide

Ah, the North-South divide. It's a contentious issue in Irish politics, but it's also a rich source of humor and linguistic difference. You see, while Northern Ireland and the Republic of Ireland may share a border and a common history, their dialects and vocabularies are as different as night and day.

Let's start with the accent. In Northern Ireland, you'll hear a distinct "Ulster" accent, which is characterized by its flat "a" sounds and heavy use of glottal stops. Meanwhile, in the Republic of Ireland, you'll hear a range of accents, from the lilting tones of the west to the sharper, more clipped sounds of Dublin.

But it's not just the accent that's different. The vocabulary is also a source of division. For example, in Northern Ireland, people often use the word "wee" to mean "small," as in "a wee cup of tea." Meanwhile, in the Republic of Ireland, the word "wee" is rarely used, and people are more likely to say "small" or "little."

Then there's the pronunciation of certain words. In Northern Ireland, the word "bath" is pronounced with a short "a" sound, while in the Republic of Ireland, it's pronounced with a long "a" sound. Similarly, in Northern Ireland, the word "grass" is pronounced with a hard "a" sound, while in the Republic of Ireland, it's pronounced with a softer, more rounded "a" sound.

Of course, there are plenty of jokes and witty observations that stem from these linguistic differences. For example, a Northern Irish person might tease their southern neighbor by saying "you sound like you're singing instead of talking," while a person from the Republic of Ireland might quip "you sound like you're chewing on your words."

Despite these differences, however, both Northern Ireland and the Republic of Ireland are united by a love of storytelling, a passion for music and dance, and a deep sense of humor. So, whether you're a "wee" Northern Irish person or a "grand" southerner, there's always something to laugh about when it comes to the North-South divide.

Chapter Seven

"Feckin' Gombeen"

LOLLY, MOOLAH & DOUGH (MONEY)

"If you want to know what God thinks of money, just look at the people he gave it to."

Irish writer and wit, Dorothy Parker

When it comes to money, the Irish have a whole lexicon of slang words and phrases that could leave outsiders scratching their heads. From **"rolling in it"** to **"loaded to the gills,"** the Irish have a colorful way of describing their finances. It's not uncommon to hear someone say they're **"skint"** or **"flat broke"** after a particularly heavy weekend of spending.

But the Irish also have a talent for finding ways to stretch their money as far as possible. If someone is being particularly stingy or cheap, you might hear them referred to as a **"tightarse"** or a **"scrooge."** And when it comes to getting a good deal, the Irish are experts at **"haggling"** or **"bargaining"** with shopkeepers to get the best possible price. At the end of the day, it's not about how much **"dosh"** you have, but how cleverly you can make it last.

If someone has **"copper-fastened"** their savings plan or investment strategy, they're likely to have a pot of gold waiting for them at the end of the rainbow. On the other hand, if someone is "scrambling for coppers," they're just barely scraping by and may have to resort to picking up odd jobs or selling items for a few euros here and there.

If someone is **"filthy rich"** they might be able to afford a private island or a solid gold bidet, and if they're **"made of money"** they seem to have an endless supply of cash. But beware of those who are **"skimming off the top"** which means taking a small amount of money from a larger amount for personal gain. At the end of the day, whether you're **"rolling in it"** or **"skint,"** it's not about the money you have, but how you choose to use it.

Rolling in it - (rol-lin in it) If someone is "rolling in it," they're flush with cash and living the high life. They've got enough moolah to splurge on luxuries like a diamond-encrusted hurley stick or a solid gold tin whistle. Example: "Did you see the size of Conor's new yacht? He's rolling in it, alright!"

Loaded to the gills - (load-ed to the gills) Similar to "rolling in it," this phrase emphasizes just how much money someone has. If someone is "loaded to the gills," they're awash with cash and can easily buy a round of drinks at the pub and still have plenty left over for a trip to the chipper. Example: "Mary's new car is a real beauty, she must be loaded to the gills!"

Skint - (skint) This Irish slang word means broke or penniless. If you're "skint," you might have to tighten your belt and pass on that round of drinks in favor of a glass of water. Example: "I can't come out tonight, I'm skint until payday."

Flat broke - (flat broke) Another way to describe someone who has no money. If you're "flat broke," you might not even be able to afford a bag of Tayto crisps or a sausage roll from the bakery. Example: "I'm flat broke, I can't even afford a bus fare."

Copper-fastened - (cop-per-fass-und) This phrase is used to describe a financial situation that is secure or guaranteed. If someone has "copper-fastened" their savings plan or investment strategy, they're sure to have a pot of gold waiting for them at the end of the rainbow. Example: "I've got my retirement fund copper-fastened, so I'm not worried about my future finances."

Scrambling for coppers - (scram-blin for cop-pers) This phrase is the opposite of "rolling in it." If someone is "scrambling for coppers," they're barely scraping by and may have to resort to odd jobs or selling items for a few euros here and there. Example: "Ever since he lost his job, he's been scrambling for coppers to pay the rent."

Filthy rich - (fil-thy rich) This phrase emphasizes just how much money someone has, to the point where it might seem excessive or even vulgar. If someone is "filthy rich," they might be able to afford a private island or a solid gold bidet. Example: "Did you hear that Conor McGregor bought a yacht for $5 million? He's filthy rich!"

Skimming off the top - (skim-min off the top) This phrase refers to someone who is taking a small amount of money from a larger amount for personal gain. It's often used in reference to corrupt politicians or business owners who are profiting off the backs of others. Example: "I suspect the boss is skimming off the top of the company profits."

Dosh - (dosh) This is another word for money, often used casually between friends. Example: "I can lend you some dosh until you get paid next week."

Moolah (moo-lah) - This nifty little term for money is believed to have originated in the United States in the early 1900s, and has since made its way to Ireland where it's now a commonly used term. So, if you're strapped for cash, just say "I'm a bit short on moolah today, sorry!" and watch as your friends come to your financial rescue (if ya lucky).

Dough (dow) - It's pronounced like the bread that you use to make a sandwich, but it's not exactly the kind of dough you want to spread butter on. No, sir! This term comes from the Irish word "dubh", which means black, and is a reference to the color of coins.

Lolly (loll-lee) - "Lolly" is an Irish slang term for money, pronounced like the candy. It's believed to have come from "lollipop" and is used in phrases like "I need more lolly to buy that pint."

Made of money (made a' money) - This phrase is used to describe someone who seems to have an endless supply of cash. If someone is "made of money," they might be able to afford to fly to the moon and back just for fun. Example: "She's always jetting off to exotic locations and buying designer clothes - she must be made of money."

Dole – This is the Irish slang term for social welfare or unemployment benefits. If someone is "on the dole," it means they're receiving financial assistance from the government. Example: "He lost his job last month and now he's on the dole."

Fiver – This is a slang term for a €5 note, commonly used in Ireland. Example: "I only have a fiver on me, can you lend me a few euros until payday?"

Gombeen (gum-been) – This is a term for a dishonest or shrewd businessperson who takes advantage of others for their own gain.

Payslip (pay-slip) – This is the document you receive from your employer detailing your pay and any deductions or contributions.

Graft (graft) – This is a term for hard work or manual labor, often used in the context of construction or farming.

Taxman (taks-man) – This is a slang term for the tax collector or the government agency responsible for collecting taxes.

Nixer (nicks-er) – This is a term for a side job or gig outside of your regular employment, often done for cash.

Chapter Eight

"I Wouldn't be Caught Dead in That!"

DRESSING TO IMPRESS

"Take the back roads instead of the highways, and you'll discover parts of Ireland that most visitors never see."

David G. Allan

When it comes to fashion, the Irish know how to look good. It's not as simple as throwing on any old outfit and walking out the door. In Ireland, putting together a complete ensemble that showcases your personal style and flair is highly valued.

Every detail matters, from carefully selecting the perfect pair of creps or runners to match your outfit to selecting the right accessories like scrunchies, bobbins, and tie-backs. And don't forget the bumbag - the ultimate accessory that can transform any outfit from drab to fab in an instant.

Of course, it's not just about what you wear; it's also about how you wear it. Irish fashion is all about attitude and confidence. You'll look good if you feel good in what you're wearing. So, don't be afraid to use bright colors, mix and match patterns, and experiment with different styles.

Whether you're going out for a night on the town, attending a formal event, or simply running errands around town, there's always a chance to show off your fashion sense. So, the next time you get ready, take a cue from the Irish and make sure you look great from head to toe. Because there is no such thing as too much style in fashion!

Threads – (thredz) This is an old-school term that refers to clothing. "That fella's got some slick threads, doesn't he?"

Gaffa tape – (gaf-uh teyp) Used to describe an outfit that is a bit rough and ready, with bits and pieces held together by tape. "She looks like she put that outfit together with gaffa tape!"

Steamin' – (steem-in) If someone looks great or is dressed to the nines, you might say they're looking steamin'. "Wow, you're looking absolutely steamin' tonight!"

Class – (klas) If something is class, it's just really cool. "Those trainers are absolutely class!"

Scobe – (skohb) This term is often used to describe someone who dresses in a flashy or showy way. "I saw a few scobes on the street today, dressed head to toe in designer gear."

Rags – (ragz) Used to describe an outfit that is a bit scruffy or unkempt. "I can't believe she left the house in those rags."

Jumper – (juhm-per) What Americans call a "sweater", the Irish call a "jumper". "I'm freezing, I need to throw on a jumper."

Nippy – (nip-ee) A little bit cold.

Rig out – (rig owt) A proper rig out is essential for a night out on the town. Whether it's a suit and tie or a flashy dress, you've got to make sure you're dressed to impress.

Savage – (sav-ij) When someone describes your outfit as savage, they're not talking about your animal instincts, they mean you look absolutely amazing. You're the king or queen of the fashion jungle.

Creps - (krehps) In Ireland, sneakers are known as creps. If you're looking to step up your shoe game, make sure you're sporting some fresh creps on your feet.

Runners – (ruhn-erz) Runners is another word for sneakers, and a staple in any Irish wardrobe. Whether you're out for a jog or just want to look cool, runners are a must-have.

Scrunchie – (skruhn-chee) The scrunchie has made a comeback and is the perfect way to tie up your luscious locks. If you're feeling lazy or just want to add some retro vibes to your outfit, throw on a scrunchie.

Bobbin – (bob-in) A bobbin is a hair accessory that keeps your braids and updos in place. It may be small, but it's mighty and keeps your hair looking fierce.

Bumbag – In Ireland, a fanny pack is known as a bumbag. It's the perfect accessory for keeping your essentials close at hand while looking stylish and cool.

Kitted out – When you're fully kitted out, you're ready for anything. Your outfit is on point, your accessories are on fleek, and you're turning heads left and right.

Looking like a ride – If someone says you're looking like a ride, take it as a huge compliment. You're oozing sex appeal and confidence in your outfit, and people can't help but be drawn to you.

"Christ, Mary, and Joseph"

It's no secret that Ireland is primarily a Catholic country, and religion has long played an important role in Irish culture. This influence can be seen in the numerous religious expressions that have entered Irish slang.

"Jesus, Mary, and Joseph" is one of the most common expressions. This phrase is frequently used as a surprise or shock exclamation and can be heard in a variety of contexts, such as **"Jaysus, Mary, and Joseph, did you hear what happened?"** or **"That was a close call, Jesus, Mary, and Joseph!"**

"Holy God," for example, can be used to express awe or disbelief, as in **"Holy God, that's a big fish!"** or **"Wait a minute, I can't believe she said that!"** **"Sweet Divine Mother of God,"** on the other hand, is typically used to express frustration or exasperation, as in **"Sweet Divine Mother of God, why won't this thing work?"** or **"Would you please pause for a moment, Sweet Divine Mother of God?"**

While these expressions may appear irreverent to some, they are simply part of Ireland's rich tapestry. Religion is a deeply ingrained part of many Irish people's identities, and these expressions serve as a way to connect with that heritage and express themselves in a uniquely Irish way.

So, don't be alarmed the next time you hear an Irish person exclaim **"Jaysus, Mary, and Joseph!"** or **"Holy God!"** or **"Sweet Divine Mother of God!"** in conversation. It's just another expressive and colorful aspect of Irish slang.

Chapter Nine

"Punchin' Above Yer Weight"

SNOGGING AND SHIFTING

"What the heart knows today the head will understand tomorrow."

James Stephens

When it comes to relationships, the Irish have their own distinct style. If you like someone, don't be afraid to **"flahulach"** a little - be generous with your attention and compliments. If you want a low-key first date, suggest going for a pint and a chat. It's a fun way to get to know each other without feeling rushed.

But be cautious, because some people are just shady businessmen who will kiss anyone they can. And even if your date turns out to be a nippy sweetie, at least you had a good time. Just make sure you're not up to anything that will land you in hot water with your mother. And if everything goes well, maybe you'll get one for the road before you part ways. To that, I say **sláinte!**

Flahulach – (fla-hool-ahk) If you catch someone flahulaching, they're flirting away to beat the band. This charming term comes from the Irish word "flaithiúlach", which means generous or hospitable. So, when someone is being flahulach, they're being generous with their attention and compliments. "He's been flahulaching with her all night," and we can't blame him – she's a catch.

Pint and a chat – A quintessential Irish first date involves meeting up for a pint and a chat in a cozy pub. "Fancy going for a pint and a chat some evening?" It's simple, relaxed, and low-pressure, which is the Irish way. Plus, it's a chance to suss out your date's taste in brews.

One for the road – Irish slang for a quick goodbye kiss before parting ways. "Come on, give me one for the road." This phrase harkens back to the Irish tradition of having a final drink or cup of tea before leaving someone's house or pub. A little smooch on the cheek is the modern version, but it's no less sweet.

Shift merchant – A shift merchant is a notorious kisser or make-out artist, always looking for their next victim. "He's a total shift merchant, he'll try it on with anyone." This phrase is a playful play on words, as "shift" in Irish can also mean a sneaky or underhanded move. Watch out for those slick talkers!

Mammy's boy – This term is used to describe a man who is overly attached to his mother, and it's usually not a compliment. "He's such a mammy's boy, he can't even make a cup of tea without her help." The term is self-explanatory, really - it refers to a man who is seen as being too close to his mother and not independent enough. Mammy's boy needs to grow up!

Loo-lah – This is a playful term for a party or social gathering that promises to be a hoot. "We had a great loo-lah last night, everyone was there." The origin of the word is uncertain, but it's thought to come from the Irish word "luí-lá," which means "bed-day" or "day of rest." No rest for the wicked, though - let's party!

Nippy Sweetie – This term is used to describe someone who is attractive but perhaps a little bit too high maintenance. "His date was a nippy sweetie - good-looking, but hard work." A high-maintenance person can be a handful, but we all know someone who's worth it. Maybe you can handle a nippy sweetie!

Heartscalded – (hart-skawl-did) This term is used to describe someone who has been deeply hurt or traumatized by a romantic relationship, often resulting in a fear of commitment or love. "She's heartscalded after her last breakup, she's not ready to date yet."

Dote – (doht) This term is used to describe someone who is cute or adorable, often used as a term of endearment. "She's such a dote, I can't resist her." This term is often used to describe a partner or significant other, and can also be used to describe a pet or child.

Culchie – (kul-chee) This term is used to describe someone from a rural or countryside area, often with a negative connotation. In the context of love or dating, it can be used to describe someone who is seen as less sophisticated or cultured than someone from a city or urban area. "She's dating a culchie, her friends can't believe it."

Fella – (fel-ah) Irish slang for a male partner or boyfriend. "She's going out with a new fella, he seems nice." This term is often used in a casual or informal way.

Wan – (Waan) Dublin slang for a woman, often used for gossip. "Sure, that wan up the street is pregnant again!"

Chapter Ten

"Fancy a Ride?"

GETTING DOWN & DIRTY (EXPLICIT!)

"If you're enough lucky to be Irish... You're lucky enough!"

Old Irish proverb

Irish slang for sex and anatomy is a vibrant tapestry woven with creative terms and colorful expressions. The Irish are renowned for their love of language, and their unique vocabulary for sexual activities and body parts is a testament to this fact. Terms such as **"ride," "shift," "minx,"** and **"horn"** are just a few of the many colorful words used by the Irish to describe sexual activities and desire. And let's not forget about **"joxer," "bollocks,"** and **"mickey,"** which are sure to make even the most stoic individuals blush.

In addition to these creative terms, the Irish also have their own unique terminology for condoms, using words like **"johnnies"** and **"yokes"** to ensure safe sex. They have also perfected the art of capturing the passion and intensity of sexual activities with phrases like **"shiftin' like rabbits"** and **"shiftin' the face off someone."** Understanding this vibrant slang is crucial for navigating Ireland's cultural landscape, whether you're a native speaker or a curious visitor. So, get ready to embrace the hilariously irreverent and colorful world of Irish sexual slang the next time you're in the Emerald Isle!

Baps – Pronounced "baps," it's a slang term for a woman's breasts. Example: "Did you see the baps on her? They were massive!"

Ride – To have sexual intercourse with someone. Example: "I rode him all night, he was fantastic!"

Shift – To kiss someone passionately with tongues. Example: "I saw them shifting in the corner, they were all over each other."

Horn – A strong sexual desire or arousal. Example: "I can't focus on anything, I have a serious horn on me."

FLOOZIE IN THE JACUZZI

Floozy – A derogatory term for a woman who is perceived as promiscuous. Example: "Don't pay attention to her, she's a floozy who sleeps around."

Joxer – (Jox-er)A slang term for an erection. Example: "He was trying to hide his joxer, but we all saw it."

Snog – To kiss someone passionately. Example: "They were snogging in the corner, it was like they were the only ones in the room."

Shiftin' like rabbits – A term used to describe couples who have frequent sexual activity. Example: "They're always shiftin' like rabbits, they can't get enough of each other."

Fanny – A slang term for a woman's genitals. Example: "She complained of a sore fanny after a night of passion."

Mickey – A slang term for a man's penis. Example: "She couldn't keep her hands off his mickey all night."

DID I, F**K!

Feck – A slang term for sexual activity. Example: "Last night was wild, we had some serious feck!"

Bird – A slang term for a woman. Example: "Look at that bird over there, she's stunning."

Shiftin' the face off someone – To kiss someone passionately and intensely. Example: "They were shiftin' the face off each other in the pub, it was like a scene from a movie."

Arse – A slang term for a person's buttocks. Example: "He's got a great arse, he must work out a lot."

Nookie – A slang term for sexual activity. Example: "I'm in the mood for some nookie, let's go back to my place."

Rodgering – A slang term for having sexual intercourse. Example: "He got caught rodgering in the back of his car by the police."

Minx – A term used to describe a woman who is sexually provocative. Example: "She's such a minx, she knows exactly what she wants."

Johnny – A slang term for a condom. Example: "I need to buy some johnnies before I go home."

Irish Folklore & Mythology

Pan:
What an Irish child first pictured when reading Greek Mythology.

Irish mythology and folklore are rich with fantastical creatures and legendary heroes that have captivated people for centuries. Let's take a closer look at some of the most intriguing characters:

The Leprechaun: Known for his love of gold and his quick wit, the Leprechaun is a mischievous little fellow who is said to be a shoemaker. According to legend, if you catch a Leprechaun, he will grant you three wishes.

The Banshee: A mournful female spirit, the Banshee is said to be a harbinger of death. In some stories, she is even said to wash the bloody clothes of those about to die.

The Pooka: The Pooka is a shape-shifting spirit who frequently takes the form of a black horse and is known for his tricks and pranks. He is rumored to be especially active around Halloween.

The Clurichaun: Like the Leprechaun, the Clurichaun is a solitary fairy who enjoys drinking and is frequently depicted as a drunkard. He is well-known for his quick temper and ability to wreak havoc and mischief.

The Selkie: A seal-like creature that can shed its skin and transform into a human, the Selkie is said to be a beautiful and enchanting creature that frequently captures humans' hearts.

The Tuatha Dé Danann: A group of mythical beings who were said to have lived in Ireland before humans arrived. They were known for their magical abilities and were credited with the construction of many of the country's ancient structures and landmarks.

The Dullahan: This headless rider carries his own severed head and is said to be a forerunner of death. According to legend, if he stops riding, someone will die.

The Changeling: A fairy child who is said to have been left in the place of a human child stolen by fairies. Changelings were thought to be sickly and frequently mischievous, and they were frequently blamed for any misfortunes that befell a family.

The Merrow: This beautiful and dangerous mermaid-like creature is known for her ability to enchant men and lure them into the sea.

And then there is **Cú Chulainn**, a legendary hero of Irish mythology known for his bravery and incredible feats of strength. He was said to have been born with all of his teeth and the ability to speak right away.

These legends have been tickling people's fancy for centuries and continue to dazzle and entertain folks from all corners of the globe. And don't be fooled by their mythological status - these characters are the backbone of Ireland's cultural heritage and have helped shape the country's distinct personality.

In short, Irish mythology and folklore are the pot of gold at the end of the rainbow - enchanting, delightful, and integral to Ireland's unique identity. So grab a pint of Guinness, sit back, and let the magic whisk you away!

Chapter Eleven

"Cramming Like a Mad Yoke"

THE CRAIC OF LEARNING

"You've got to do your own growing, no matter how tall your father was."

Irish Proverb

Oh, the Irish know how to get educated! From ancient scriptoriums to the modern-day lecture halls of Trinity College, Irish education has always been of the highest quality. And, thanks to their own slang, the Irish can make even the most boring lectures sound like a fun night at the pub! So, gather your pens and paper, get to work, and learn some Irish education jargon.

Do you require additional assistance with your studies? No problem, just go grind and you'll be fine in no time. However, if you're a **"skiver"** who is constantly sleeping in, you might end up in a **"blackboard jungle"** of a classroom! And don't even try to **"shtudy"** the night before an exam; you'll be cramming like an eejit until the wee hours of the morning.

But, hey, if you're a real **"schkoolbag"** who enjoys learning, your outstanding essay on Irish history might just win you a **"gradam"**. And if you want to go to university, make sure you hit those point targets or you'll be left out in the cold. So, whether you're a new or experienced lecturer, there's always something new to learn in the wild and wonderful world of Irish education jargon!

Bluffer – (BLUH-fur) Someone who's good at talking their way out of a situation or pretending to know more than they actually do. Example: "He didn't do any of the reading, but he's such a bluffer that he still got an A on the essay." Origin: The word "bluffer" comes from the verb "to bluff," which means to deceive or mislead someone by pretending to be confident or knowledgeable.

Gaffa tape degree – (GAH-fuh tape DEE-gree) A degree that has been achieved through practical experience rather than academic qualifications. Example: "He may not have a degree, but he's got a gaffa tape degree in engineering from years of fixing machinery." Origin: The term "gaffa tape" refers to a brand of duct tape that's commonly used in construction and engineering. The phrase "gaffa tape degree" is often used to describe someone who has gained expertise through hands-on experience rather than formal education.

Grind - (GRYND) A private tutoring session for a student who needs extra help with their studies. For example: "I'm really struggling with math, so I've started going to grinds once a week."

Cram - (KRAM) The act of studying intensively before an exam or assignment deadline. For example: "I'm going to be up all night cramming for my history exam tomorrow."

Skivers - (SKY-vurs) Students who skip classes or lectures. For example: "The teacher caught a few skivers hanging out at the mall instead of attending their lecture."

Freshers - (FRESH-urs) First-year students at university or college. For example: "I remember when I was a fresher, everything was so new and exciting."

Blackboard Jungle - (BLAK-bord JUNG-ul) A term used to describe a difficult or unruly classroom environment. For example: "The teacher really had her work cut out for her with that blackboard jungle of a class."

Lecturer - (LEK-cher-ur) A professor or teacher at a university or college. For example: "My lecturer for English Lit is really passionate about the subject."

Bunking off - (BUNK-ing off) The act of skipping school without permission. For example: "I got in trouble for bunking off last week to go to the beach."

Gradam - (GRAH-dum) An Irish language word meaning "prize" or "award". For example: "I won a gradam for my essay on Irish history."

Points - (POYNTS) The number of points a student needs to obtain in their final exams in order to qualify for admission to university or college. For example: "I need to get at least 500 points to get into my first choice university."

Shtudy - (SHTUH-dee) This is a common way of saying "study" in Irish slang, usually pronounced with a heavy emphasis on the "sh" sound. For example, "I have to do some shtudy for my exams tomorrow."

Schkoolbag - (SKOOL-bag) This is a playful term used to describe someone who's particularly studious or obsessed with learning. For example, "She's always got her head in a book, she's a real schkoolbag."

Buck Eejit - (EE-jit) This is a term used to describe someone who's being particularly foolish or acting stupidly. It's not necessarily related to education, but it's a term you're likely to hear in any group of Irish students. For example, "I can't believe he didn't show up for his own exam, what an eejit!"

Béarlóir - (BAYR-loh-eer) A person who speaks English exclusively, often used as a derogatory term in Irish-speaking communities. Example: "I can't believe they're such a béarlóir, they didn't even attempt to speak Irish!" Origin: The word "Béarlóir" is a combination of the Irish words "Béarla" (English) and "Labhair" (speak). It's believed to have originated during the Gaelic Revival in the late 19th and early 20th centuries, when there was a push to revive the Irish language and culture.

GAA Stars

The Gaelic Athletic Association, or GAA as we like to call it, is an institution in Ireland. It is more than a sports organization; it is a way of life. The GAA is all about hurling, Gaelic football, and the devoted fans who support these sports with zeal and devotion.

To begin, consider hurling, an ancient Irish sport that has been practiced for over 3,000 years. Consider a hybrid of field hockey and lacrosse, with a dash of medieval warfare thrown in for good measure. That's throwing. It's intense, physical, and not for the faint of heart.

Then there's Gaelic football, a cross between soccer, rugby, and American football. It is played on a rectangular field with a ball that resembles a soccer ball crossed with a volleyball. The goal of the game is to score a point by kicking the ball through the opponent's goalposts or over the crossbar. It's a game of skill, strategy, and endurance.

But the GAA is about more than just sports. It's also about the devoted fans who back them up. The GAA has its own culture, with its own traditions and rituals. The GAA is all about community and camaraderie, from the singing of the national anthem before the game to the post-game celebrations in the local pub.

Let us not forget the players themselves. They are heroes, not just athletes. GAA players are idolized in Ireland, much like rock stars. They represent their counties on the field, bringing glory and honor to their communities. It's no surprise that GAA games are among the most intense and emotional sporting events on the planet.

So, whether you're a die-hard GAA supporter or simply curious about this unique Irish institution, one thing is certain: the GAA is more than just a sports organization. It represents Irish culture, history, and identity. It's about coming together as a community and celebrating what makes us unique.

Chapter Twelve

"Gardaí on Me Arse!"

LAW & ORDER

"There is no such thing as bad publicity except your own obituary."

Brendan Behan

Ah, you're in for a real craic learning about the unique world of Irish law and order! From the Garda Síochána to the courts and legal jargon, the Emerald Isle has its own peculiar lexicon when it comes to matters of justice. Don't be a **"gawk"** and miss out on the chance to learn about the quirky slang and colloquialisms used in Irish law.

Watch out for those **"skangers"** lurking around the corner, as we delve into the world of Irish law and crime jargon. The Guards are always on the lookout for these troublemakers, keeping the peace and protecting the citizens of Ireland. And if you need a **"yoke"** for your latest heist, you might want to brush up on your Irish slang for law and crime. But don't be a **"gombeen"** and get caught like a real **"scofflaw"**, or you might find yourself in a real **"blackboard jungle"** of a courtroom. So, grab a pint of the black stuff, put on your best legal wig, and let's get started!

Juke – To steal or rob. For example: "I heard he juke the corner shop last night." The origin of the word 'juke' is uncertain, but it's thought to have come from the Irish word 'dúcadh', which means 'robbery' or 'theft'. In Irish slang, 'juke' is often used to refer to stealing or robbing, especially in a quick and surreptitious manner. It can also be used in the context of cheating or trickery, such as in the phrase "he juked me out of my money".

Gawk – (gawk) To look at something or someone in a suspicious manner. For example: "The guards were giving us gawks as we walked past." The word 'gawk' is believed to come from the Irish word 'gáirc,' which means to stare or gaze intently. It's often used in the context of criminal activity, where someone might be giving another person a suspicious look.

Yoke – (yohk) A general term for an object or thing, often used when the speaker can't remember the actual name. For example: "Hand me that yoke over there, will you?" The word 'yoke' is used in a variety of contexts in Irish slang, but it's often used to refer to something that's being used in the commission of a crime, such as a tool or a weapon.

Skanger – (SKAYN-jer) A derogatory term for someone who's seen as a troublemaker or a criminal. For example: "Watch out for those skangers hanging around the corner." The word 'skanger' comes from the Irish word 'scairteoir,' which means a scatterbrained or reckless person. It's often used to describe someone who's involved in criminal activity or anti-social behavior.

The Guards – (the gards) The police. For example: "The guards are always hanging around here, keeping an eye on things." This term is pretty self-explanatory, but it's worth noting that the Irish police force is officially known as An Garda Síochána, which means 'the guardians of the peace.'

STACY SPENT DAYS
WAITING FOR THE LONG FINGER.

Long Finger – (long fin-ger) This phrase is used to describe someone who is a thief or who tends to take things that don't belong to them. Example: "Be careful leaving your phone on the table around him, he's a bit of a Long Finger." When it comes to time, "Long Finger" is used to describe someone who takes a long time to complete a task or arrive at a destination. Example: "He said he'd be here ten minutes ago, he's always a Long Finger."

Mickey Finn – A drink that's been spiked with a drug or other substance. For example: "I think someone put something in my drink, I feel really weird." The origin of the term 'Mickey Finn' is unclear, but it's thought to come from a

Chicago bartender who would drug his customers and then rob them in the early 1900s. It's now used to describe any drink that's been spiked.

Scofflaw – Someone who habitually breaks the law. For example: "He's a real scofflaw, always getting into trouble with the guards." The word 'scofflaw' was actually coined during Prohibition in America, when people would break the law by drinking alcohol. It's a combination of the words 'scoff' (to mock or ridicule) and 'law.'

Divil – (DIV-uhl) A mischievous or troublesome person. For example: "He's a real divil, always getting up to no good." The word 'divil' is a common Irish pronunciation of the word 'devil.' It's often used to describe someone who's mischievous or troublesome.

Skite – to hit or strike someone, often used in the context of a physical altercation. For example: "He skited me in the face and then ran off before I could do anything."

Langer – A foolish or annoying person. For example: "Stop acting like a langer and get your act together." The word 'langer' comes from the Irish word 'langar,' which means a clumsy or uncoordinated person. It's often used to describe someone who's being foolish or annoying.

Chapter Thirteen

"Full of Cold"

AS SICK AS A DOG

Here's to health and prosperity,
To you and all your posterity.
And them that doesn't drink with sincerity,
That they may be damned for all eternity!

Irish toast

When you think of Ireland, images of lively pubs and hearty cuisine might come to mind. However, the Irish also have a strong focus on health and fitness. Whether it's hiking, surfing, hurling, or Gaelic football, staying active and fit is a fundamental part of Irish culture. And like any culture, there's a whole host of slang words and phrases used to describe health and wellness. So, let's put on our hiking boots and dive into the world of Irish slang for health and fitness because the Irish value staying fit and healthy.

In addition to traditional Irish greetings like **"Céad míle fáilte,"** which reflects the warm hospitality associated with Irish healthcare, there are other phrases that celebrate health and wellness. For example, the common Irish toast, **"Sláinte"** means "health" or "good health." On the other hand, if you're feeling exhausted or run down, you might describe yourself as feeling **"banjaxed."** And while **"fluthered"** is often used to describe being drunk, it can also refer to feeling feverish or unwell. So, let's learn some new Irish slang words and phrases to describe health and fitness and celebrate the Irish way of life.

Céad míle fáilte – (kayd mee-luh fawl-chuh) When you hear this traditional Irish greeting, you know you're in for a warm welcome. "Céad míle fáilte" means "a hundred thousand welcomes" and is often associated with the kindness and hospitality of Irish healthcare providers. Example: "As soon as I walked into the clinic, I was greeted with a céad míle fáilte. It instantly put me at ease."

Bád – (bawd) While "bád" is the Irish word for boat, it's also used to describe feeling sick or under the weather. Example: "I think I ate something bad last night, I feel like bád today. I might need to call in sick."

Dose – (dohs) If you're feeling a bit under the weather with a cold or other mild illness, you might describe it as a dose. Example: "I've got a bit of a dose today, my nose won't stop running and my throat is sore." In northern parts of Ireland, this term can refer to a person being irritating.

Fluthered – (fluh-thurd) While commonly used to describe being drunk, "fluthered" can also refer to feeling feverish or generally unwell. Example: "I think I'm coming down with something, I feel fluthered and my head is pounding."

Gowl – (goul) A general term for someone who's being annoying or frustrating, but it can also be used to describe someone who's not taking care of their health. Example: "My boss has been such a gowl lately, always micromanaging everything. And he's not even taking his vitamins to stay healthy."

Pox – (poks) While it can be used to describe someone who's unpleasant or irritating, "pox" can also be used to describe an illness or infection. Example: "I caught a pox of a cold last week, and it's still lingering. I can't seem to shake it."

The Runs – (the runz) A slang term for diarrhea or other stomach issues, often used in a comical way. Example: "I can't make it into work today, I've got the runs something fierce. I need to stay close to the bathroom."

Knackered – (nak-erd) A term used to describe feeling extremely tired or worn out, often as a result of an illness or strenuous activity. Example: "I was out sick for a week with the flu, and now I'm completely knackered. I can barely make it up the stairs."

Snotser – (snot-ser) A term used to describe someone who's constantly sick or sniffling, often due to allergies or a weak immune system. Example: "He's always sneezing and blowing his nose, he's a real snotser."

Whist – (wist) A term used to describe feeling healthy or well, often after recovering from an illness or injury. Example: "After a week of rest and lots of fluids, I'm finally feeling whist again. It's amazing how quickly your health can bounce back."

Chapter Fourteen

"Bagsy Front Seat!"

HITTIN" THE ROAD

"May your troubles be less and your blessings be more, and nothing but happiness come through your door."

Irish Blessing

The Irish may have their own quirky slang for transportation, but with the breathtaking views of the Emerald Isle, you might not want to rush to get anywhere. Take a **"toodle"** in a **"shtoop"** or flag down a **"hackney"** for a leisurely ride, just be sure not to get **"clamped!"** And if you're feeling adventurous, go for a **"shkelp"** in the hills, but be careful not to end up in the back of beyond.

If you're a tourist, don't forget to take the **"Ring of Kerry"** and visit the **"holey stones"** but be prepared for crowds - it might just be jammers! And when it's time to say goodbye, make sure to wish your fellow travelers **"slán abhaile!"** With all the unique transportation lingo and stunning scenery, getting around Ireland is truly a wild ride!

Toodle – (TOO-dul) Irish slang for a leisurely drive or ride, often taken to enjoy the scenery. "Let's take a toodle along the coast and stop for some photos." This word is a variation of the English word "tootle", which means to drive or ride slowly and leisurely.

Shtoop – (sh-TOOP) Irish slang for a cheap or old-fashioned bicycle. "I'm thinking of getting a shtoop to save some money on my commute." This word comes from the Irish word "stuab", which means a narrow or crooked path.

Hackney – Irish slang for a taxi or cab. "We need to get a hackney to the pub, no one wants to be the designated driver." This word comes from the name of the town of Hackney in London, where horse-drawn carriages were once a popular mode of transportation.

Holey stones – Irish slang for the iconic Cliffs of Moher. "We couldn't resist taking some selfies at the holey stones, the view was incredible." This phrase comes from the Irish name for the cliffs, "Aillte an Mhothair", which means "cliffs of the ruin" or "cliffs of the fort".

Slán abhaile – (slawn uh-WAH-luh) Irish slang for "safe home", a common farewell used when someone is leaving. "Thanks for having us over, slán abhaile!" This phrase comes from the Irish language and is used to wish someone a safe journey home.

Shkelp – Irish slang for walking or hiking, often used in the context of a leisurely walk in the countryside. "Let's go for a shkelp through the woods and enjoy the autumn colors." This word comes from the Irish word "sealbh", which means to possess or hold.

Clamped – Irish slang for having a car immobilized by a parking enforcement authority, often used in the context of illegally parked cars. "I can't believe I got clamped outside my own house, it's so frustrating." This word comes from the idea of a clamp being placed on the wheel of a car to prevent it from moving.

Back of beyond – noun, a remote or isolated location. "Their farmhouse is in the back of beyond, we had to drive for hours to get there." This phrase is used to describe a place that's far from civilization or hard to reach.

Haul – verb, to transport goods or drive over a long distance. "He's been hauling cattle across the country for years, he knows every road like the back of his hand." This word is often used in the context of long-distance trucking or shipping.

Ring of Kerry – This term is used to refer to a scenic drive around the Iveragh Peninsula in County Kerry. For example, "We did the Ring of Kerry and stopped at all the viewpoints, it was breathtaking." The route is popular with tourists and features stunning landscapes, charming villages, and historic landmarks.

Hatch - (hach) Irish slang for the trunk or boot of a car. "Can you put the bags in the hatch before we hit the road?"

Booze bus - (booz buz) Irish slang for a bus that is often used for pub crawls or other drinking events. "We're taking the booze bus to the stag party tonight."

Shank's mare - (SHANKZ mar) Irish slang for walking or traveling on foot, often used in the context of not having access to other modes of transportation. "The car's in the shop, so we're on Shank's mare for the next few days."

Sleeper - (SLEEp-er) Irish slang for an overnight train or bus, often used for long-distance travel. "We're taking the sleeper to Cork tonight to save on accommodation."

Stop the lights - (STOP thuh lites) Irish slang for an expression of surprise or disbelief, often used in the context of seeing something while traveling. "Stop the lights, would you look at that view!"

Kissing Rocks and Other Absurdities: A Comical Look at Irish Tourism

When it comes to tourist attractions, the Blarney Stone isn't the only rock with a reputation in Ireland. Have you heard of the Kissing Rocks of Killorglin? That's right, there's a pair of rocks in County Kerry that supposedly bring good luck to couples who kiss while standing on them. And of course, like the Blarney Stone, there's a steady stream of tourists who come to take a smoochy photo op on the rocks.

But let's be real, the Kissing Rocks are just another absurdity in the world of Irish tourism. Sure, they might be a cute spot for a photo, but there's no magical power behind them. And yet, the tourists keep coming, eager to add another quirky Irish experience to their vacation itinerary.

And speaking of quirky Irish experiences, have you ever heard of the Puck Fair? It's a festival held in the town of Killorglin every August, where a wild mountain goat is crowned king and paraded through the streets. The origins of the festival are unclear, but it's been going strong for over 400 years.

Of course, like any good Irish festival, there's plenty of music, dancing, and drinking involved. And if you're feeling adventurous, you can even try some of the local delicacies, like fried black pudding or a pint of Guinness with a dash of blackcurrant juice (known as a "blackcurrant Guinness").

But for all the absurdities of Irish tourism, there are also plenty of authentic and awe-inspiring sights to see. From the stunning Cliffs of Moher to the hauntingly beautiful Glendalough, Ireland is a country filled with natural wonders.

And let's not forget about the rich history and culture that Ireland has to offer. From the ancient ruins of Newgrange to the vibrant city of Dublin, there's no shortage of museums, galleries, and historical sites to explore.

So the next time you're planning a trip to Ireland, don't just focus on the absurdities and tourist traps. Take the time to truly appreciate all that this beautiful country has to offer, and maybe you'll even come away with a bit of the "gift of gab" after all.

Chapter Fifteen

"Jigs and Reels"

THE MUSIC SCENE

"May your heart be light and happy, may your smile be big and wide, and may your pockets always have a coin or two inside!"

Irish Proverb

Ah, Irish music, and the craic, they go together like peas and carrots - or Guinness and a good pub, for that matter. For centuries, the fiddle and tin whistle have been lifting the roof of many a lively session, with generations of music enthusiasts passing down their melodies and stories from one to the next. But the Irish don't just stick to tradition and heritage; they know how to bring down the house on the world stage, too. Just look at musical icons like Van Morrison and the Pogues, who bring their own distinct flavor to the scene.

But don't think for a second that the Irish are content to just listen to music. Whether it's the **"bodhrán"** drumming out a rhythm at a traditional session or the electric guitar wailing away at a rock concert, the Irish have a long history of making their own music. So grab your favorite instrument and prepare to be immersed in the wild and wonderful world of Irish music. And keep an eye out for the **"sesh gremlins"** - those enthusiastic folks who take their love of music sessions a little too seriously. **Sláinte!**"

Trad - (trad) When Irish people refer to "trad", they're talking about traditional Irish music. It's a celebration of the tunes, songs and dance that have been handed down through the generations, and a nod to the musicians who have kept them alive. Example: "I love heading to the local pub for some good trad music. It's the perfect way to unwind after a long week."

Ceili - (kay-lee) The word "ceili" literally means "gathering", but in Ireland it's synonymous with traditional group dancing. Ceilis can take place at weddings, community events or even in pubs, and everyone is welcome to join in. Example: "I'm looking forward to the ceili tonight. It's always a great night of music and dancing."

Sessioneer - (sess-un-eer) This is the person who's always in search of a good music session. They know the best spots for live music, and will happily lead the charge in starting up an impromptu jam session. Example: "We need a sessioneer to get this party started. Who's up for some tunes?"

Tradhead - (trad-hed) A tradhead is someone who is passionate about traditional Irish music. They're likely to have a vast collection of recordings, attend concerts and festivals, and may even play an instrument themselves. Example: "Sarah is a real tradhead. She knows all the lyrics to the old songs and loves nothing more than a good session with her friends."

Pub singing - (pub sing-ing) It's not unusual to find yourself singing along to some old Irish tunes in a pub late at night. Pub singing sessions are spontaneous and anyone can join in, whether they're a seasoned performer or a nervous newbie. Example: "Last night we ended up in a pub singing until the early hours. It was one of the best nights I've had in ages."

Sesh Gremlin - (sesh greml-in) A sesh gremlin is someone who takes their love for partying to the extreme. They're always the last one standing, looking for another pint and another tune, even when everyone else has gone home. Example: "Don't invite Sean to the sesh, he's a bit of a sesh gremlin and will keep us up all night."

Feis - (fesh) A feis is a traditional Irish music festival that takes place in the summertime. It's a celebration of music, dance and culture, and a great opportunity to experience live performances. Example: "I can't wait for the Feis next weekend, I've got my dancing shoes ready."

Whistle player - (whis-tle play-er) The tin whistle is a popular instrument in traditional Irish music, and a great way to get started as a musician. If you're a fan of Irish music, you might want to try your hand at playing the whistle yourself.

Example: "I'm learning to play the tin whistle so I can join in the sessions with the other whistle players."

Seisiun - (se-shun) A seisiun is another word for a traditional Irish music session, where musicians come together to play and celebrate the music. These gatherings can be more formal and structured than impromptu sessions, and a great way to experience the talent and skill of Irish musicians. Example: "The seisiun last night was incredible. The musicians were amazing, and I learned so much about the history of the music."

Danny Boy - (dan-ee boy) "Danny Boy" is a classic Irish ballad that's known and loved around the world. It's a staple of many Irish music sessions and concerts, and a song that will bring a tear to many an eye. Example: "We finished off the night with a rendition of Danny Boy. There wasn't a dry eye in the house."

Ceili band – (kay-lee) If you're into Irish dancing, you're probably familiar with ceili bands, which are groups of musicians who play music specifically for ceili dances. These bands often feature instruments like the fiddle, accordion, and bodhran. So, put on your dancing shoes and get ready for a great time!

Bodhran – (bow-rawn) Speaking of the bodhran, this is a traditional Irish drum that's played with a stick or a hand. It's often used in Irish music to provide a rhythmic accompaniment to other instruments like the fiddle and the accordion. It's not just a drum, it's a heartbeat that keeps the music going.

Uilleann pipes – (ill-un pipes) These are a type of bagpipes that are commonly used in Irish music. They have a distinctive sound and are often featured in slow, mournful tunes as well as faster, more lively tunes. The haunting sound of the Uilleann pipes will send shivers down your spine.

Póg mo thóin – (pogue muh ho-in) This is a not-so-polite phrase that means "kiss my arse." It's often used in a playful, teasing way and is sometimes shouted at a band or performer if they're not playing a song that the audience wants to hear. But don't take it too seriously, it's all in good fun!

Riverdance – This is a popular Irish dance show that was first performed in 1994. It features a mix of traditional Irish music and dance, as well as more modern elements, and it's been seen by millions of people around the world. It's a high-energy celebration of Irish culture that will have you tapping your feet and clapping your hands in no time.

Claddagh ring – This is a traditional Irish ring that features two hands holding a heart, with a crown on top. The hands represent friendship, the heart represents love, and the crown represents loyalty. It's a popular symbol of Irish heritage and culture, and it's often worn as a wedding ring or a symbol of friendship.

Céilidh – (kay-lee) This is a type of traditional Irish social gathering that involves music, dance, and storytelling. It's a great way to experience Irish culture and to meet new people, and it's often held in pubs or community centers.

Dublin Music Scene in the 1960s

During the 1960s, the Irish music scene in Dublin was vibrant, creative, and rebellious. It was a time when young Irish musicians were drawing inspiration from The Beatles, The Rolling Stones, and other British bands to create their own distinct sound.

The Dubliners, The Chieftains, and The Wolfe Tones were at the forefront of the scene, performing in pubs and clubs all over the city. Music was more than just a form of entertainment for them; it was a way of life. Dubliners would gather to listen to music, dance, sing, and drink the night away, all while taking in the sounds and slang of the music scene.

"Craic," which means "fun" or "entertainment," is one of the most well-known Irish slang terms from this era. It was frequently used to describe the lively atmosphere of music sessions, where people would gather to enjoy the music, have a few drinks, and tell stories. "The craic was mighty last night at the pub," for example, "we had some great music and plenty of pints!"

Another popular slang term at the time was **"session,"** which refers to a gathering of musicians who come together to play traditional Irish music. It's still a popular phrase today, especially in the pub scene. "We're going to the pub later for a session; there should be some great traditional music tonight!"

Not to mention **"sláinte,"** which translates to "cheers" in Irish. It's a common phrase used with friends when drinking and has become a staple of Irish pub culture. So, the next time you're clinking glasses with your mates, be sure to raise your glass and say **"sláinte!"**

But it's not just the words that have been influenced by 1960s music. The way people speak has also been influenced. Many Irish slang phrases have the same intonation and rhythm as traditional Irish music. The phrase **"fair play,"** for example, is frequently spoken with a lilting, sing-song accent that mirrors the rhythms of Irish music.

Aside from the music itself, the musicians of the time were influential in shaping Irish slang. Many of them were rebels and outsiders, and their music and language reflected their rebellious spirit and anti-establishment attitude. Slang was used to express their individuality and to rebel against social norms.

The Dubliners' hit song "The Wild Rover," for example, made the phrase **"three sheets to the wind"** popular. It is used to describe someone who is extremely inebriated and unable to walk straight. Meanwhile, the term **"jive"** was originally used to describe a type of dance in the Irish music scene, evolving into a term for any type of party or social gathering.

The impact of Dublin's Irish music scene in the 1960s can still be felt today. Many Irish slang phrases have become commonplace not only in Ireland, but around the world.

Chapter Sixteen
"Donkey's Years"
TIME FLIES

"May you be at the gates of heaven an hour before the devil knows you're dead!"

Irish Proverb

Time is a wonderful thing in Ireland. However, if you are not from around here, you may find yourself a little lost in translation when it comes to the local lingo. That's because the Irish have their own way of describing the passage of time, which is full of colorful phrases and slang that will make you smile.

Consider the **"grand stretch in the evenings."** This expression refers to the longer days of spring and summer, when the sun sets later and people can spend more time outside. How about **"donkey's years,"** a term used to describe a very long period of time, typically spanning several decades? It's one of many odd phrases you might hear in an Irish pub or on the street.

But don't be fooled by seemingly simple words like "**minute**" or "**half.**" These words can take on entirely new meaning in Irish slang. Saying you'll be there in a "**minute**" could actually mean 10 or 15 minutes, whereas "**half**" refers to 30 minutes past the hour. And if someone promises to be "**back in a jiffy,**" don't expect them to be gone for long.

So, whether you want to blend in with the locals or just brush up on your Irish slang, there's no better time than the present to explore the world of time-related phrases and sayings.

Jiffy – (jif-ee) This word is used to describe a very short amount of time, usually just a few seconds. You might hear someone say, "I'll be back in a jiffy!" Example: "Hold on a jiffy, I just need to grab my keys."

Yonks – (yonks) This word is used to describe a very long time, usually several years or even decades. You might hear someone say, "I haven't seen her in yonks!" Example: "I haven't been to that restaurant in yonks, let's go check it out."

Minute – (min-it) In Irish slang, "minute" can actually mean quite a long time! If someone says they'll be there in a minute, it might actually mean 10 or 15 minutes. Example: "I'll be ready in a minute, just need to finish getting dressed."

Ten past – (ten past) This is how some Irish people describe a time that is 10 minutes past the hour. For example, if it's 2:10, someone might say "It's ten past two." Example: "I'll meet you at the café at ten past three."

Half – (haf) Similar to "ten past," this is how some Irish people describe a time that is 30 minutes past the hour. For example, if it's 3:30, someone might say "It's half three." Example: "Let's meet for lunch at half one."

Donkey's years – (don-keys yeers) This phrase is used to describe a very long time, usually several decades. You might hear someone say, "I haven't been to that pub in donkey's years!" Example: "I haven't seen my cousin in donkey's years, we should catch up."

The witching hour – (witch-ing our) This phrase is used to describe midnight or the early hours of the morning, when supernatural activity is said to be at its strongest. You might hear someone say, "I was up until the witching hour last night." Example: "I always feel a bit spooked when it's the witching hour."

Punctual as a Swiss watch – (pungk-choo-al as a swis wotch) This phrase is used to describe someone who is always on time. You might hear someone say, "Oh, he's always punctual as a Swiss watch!" Example: "My boss is punctual as a Swiss watch, we never have to wait for him."

Eejit o'clock – (ee-jit o-clock) This phrase is used to describe a time when someone does something silly or foolish. For example, if someone wakes up very late in the day, you might say "Looks like you got up at eejit o'clock." Example: "I accidentally set my alarm for 3am instead of 3pm, I woke up at eejit o'clock."

Chapter Seventeen

"Freezing me Balls Off"

FOUR SEASONS IN A DAY

"We may have bad weather in Ireland, but the sun shines in the hearts of the people and that keeps us all warm."

Marianne Williamson

T alking about the weather in Ireland is practically a national pastime. Rain or shine, it's always a hot topic. When the rain starts falling, the Irish have a unique way of looking at it - they call it a **"soft day."** But don't let the gentle-sounding name fool you - with Ireland's reputation for experiencing all four seasons in one day, it's best to keep an eye on the sky and carry a brolly just in case.

Despite the unpredictable weather, the Irish are a resilient bunch, and they don't let a little rain get in the way of their plans. As the saying goes, "there's no such thing as bad weather, only unsuitable clothing." And when it's really coming down, forget about **"raining cats and dogs"** - in

Ireland, we say it's **"lashing."** It's like the heavens have opened up and someone's turned on a hose.

So if you're visiting Ireland, be prepared for anything - the sun could be shining one minute and the next minute you could be caught in a downpour. But don't worry, the locals are used to it and always happy to chat about the weather forecast. Just remember to bring your raincoat or umbrella if you plan to venture out during a **"lashing."**

Lashing - (lash-in) Lashing is used to describe heavy rainfall, typically in a short period of time. Example: "I was just out for a walk when the heavens opened and it started lashing down. I was soaked in seconds!"

Sunny spells - (sun-ee spels) Sunny spells refers to brief periods of sunshine that occur between cloudy or overcast weather. Example: "It's been a pretty cloudy day, but there have been some sunny spells here and there which have been nice."

Feckin' Baltic - (fek-in ball-tick) Feckin' Baltic is used to describe extremely cold weather. Feckin' is a mild curse word in Ireland, similar to "freaking" or "bloody". Example: "I don't know how anyone could go outside in this feckin' Baltic weather! My fingers are numb after just a few minutes."

Soft Day - (sawft day) Soft Day is a term used to describe a cloudy, misty or drizzly day. It's a common phrase in Ireland and is often used to describe the country's typically damp weather. Example: "Ah, it's just a soft day today. Nothing too heavy, but it's enough to make you damp and miserable."

Grand stretch in the evenings - (grawnch-stretch-in-tha-eev-nins) Grand stretch in the evenings is used to describe the longer daylight hours in the summer months. It refers to the fact that the evenings feel longer and more relaxed when it's still bright outside. Example: "I love this time of year. There's a grand stretch in the evenings and it's great to be able to go for a walk after work when it's still bright outside."

Muggy - (mug-ee) Muggy is used to describe hot, humid weather that makes you feel sweaty and uncomfortable. Example: "I can't stand this muggy weather. It's like a sauna outside!"

Fierce Wind - (fi-ers wind) Fierce Wind is used to describe strong, gusty winds that can be difficult to stand or walk in. Example: "I was nearly blown over by the fierce wind when I was walking to the shops. It's really picking up now."

Dry Shite - (dry shoit) Dry Shite is used to describe a day that's dull and uneventful, typically without any significant weather activity. Example: "Nothing's happening today, it's just dry shite. I wish something would happen to break up the monotony."

Pissin' - (piss-in) Pissin' is used to describe heavy rain, similar to lashing. Example: "It's been pissin' it down all day. I can't wait for this weather to pass."

Fine Aul Day - (fine aul day) Fine Aul Day is a term used to describe a pleasant, sunny day. Example: "It's a fine aul day today, I think I'll head to the beach and make the most of it!"

Baltic Snaw - (ball-tick snaw) Baltic Snaw is used to describe very cold and snowy weather conditions. Example: "It's Baltic snaw outside today, I wouldn't be caught dead without my coat and scarf!"

Chapter Eighteen

"Slán go fóill"

A LITTLE EXTRA

"May your heart be light and happy, may your smile be big and wide, and may your pockets always have a coin or two inside!"

Irish Proverb

As we approach the culmination of our captivating and idiosyncratic odyssey into the universe of Irish slang, it's with a touch of melancholy that we reveal the last remaining terms. These final few expressions contribute further to the kaleidoscope of vivid and evocative phrases that define the Irish dialect. Each phrase is a unique thread that weaves into the rich tapestry of colloquialisms, creating a fabric of language that reflects the character and humor of the Irish people.

Although our journey is drawing to a close, the memories and impressions of our time spent delving into the depths of Irish slang will linger on. The humor, wit, and quirkiness of this distinctive vernacular have added an unmistakable charm to our travels, and we hope that you too have enjoyed the experience.

From **"craic"** to **"banjaxed,"** we've explored a plethora of expressions that are both charming and irreverent. We've laughed at the absurdity of some phrases and marveled at the creativity behind others. But most importantly, we've gained an appreciation for the depth and richness of the Irish language and the culture it represents. Not to worry as there are few more terms you should know.

Chancer – (Chan-Sir) A term that means someone who is a scheming opportunist, often used when someone is about to take a risk. "Oh, we got a chancer here!"

Deadly buzz – (DEHD-lee buhz) A term used to describe a really exciting or thrilling experience in Ireland. It's a phrase that's commonly used to convey a sense of exhilaration or high spirits. Example: "Going on that rollercoaster was a deadly buzz, I loved it."

Pure savage – (PYOOR sah-vij) A term used to describe something that is really amazing or incredible in Ireland. It's a phrase that's commonly used to express admiration or awe. Example: "That sunset was pure savage, the colors were breathtaking."

Deadly sound – (DEHD-lee sownd) A term used to describe someone who is really cool, friendly and trustworthy in Ireland. It's a phrase that's commonly used to convey a sense of respect or admiration. Example: "He's a deadly sound guy, always up for a laugh."

Mighty - (MYE-tee) A term used to describe something that is really good or excellent in Ireland. It's a phrase that's commonly used to express satisfaction or approval. Example: "The food at that restaurant was mighty, I'd go back again."

Sorted – (SAWRT-id) A term used to describe a situation that has been successfully resolved or taken care of in Ireland. It's a phrase that's commonly used to convey a sense of relief or accomplishment. Example: "Thanks for your help, everything is sorted now."

Yer man/yer wan – (yur man/wan) A term used to refer to a person whose name you can't remember in Ireland. It's a phrase that's commonly used to avoid using someone's name when you can't recall it. Example: "Yer man from the pub was telling me about his travels."

Tip-top – (tip-top) A term used to describe something that is really good or excellent in Ireland. It's a phrase that's commonly used to convey a sense of satisfaction or approval. Example: "The service at that restaurant was tip-top, we had a great experience."

Shitehawk - (SHYT-hawk) A term used to describe someone who is lazy or unreliable, particularly in a work context. Example: "He's always late, he's a shitehawk." The origins of the word are unclear, but it may come from the Irish word "síochán," meaning peace.

SHITEHAWK

Sorted for chips – (SAWRT-id fohr chips) A term used to describe being in a good situation in Ireland. It's a phrase that's commonly used to convey a sense of contentment or satisfaction. Example: "I've got a steady job and good friends, I'm sorted for chips."

Jackeen - (JAK-een) A term used to describe someone from Dublin, often used in a derogatory way by people from other parts of Ireland. Example: "He's a bit of a jackeen, isn't he?" The term may have originated from the name "Jack," which was a common name in Dublin in the 19th century.

Cracker – (KRAK-ur) A term used to describe something that is really good or impressive in Ireland. It's a phrase that's commonly used to express enthusiasm or appreciation. Example: "That joke was a cracker, I couldn't stop laughing."

Happy as a pig in shite – (HA-pee az uh pig in shoit) A term used to express extreme happiness or contentment in Ireland. It's a phrase that's commonly used to convey a sense of joy or satisfaction. Example: "He got his dream job and he's happy as a pig in shite."

Gobshite – (GAHB-shyt) A term used to describe someone who talks nonsense or says stupid things in Ireland. It's a popular phrase, often used in a lighthearted way. Example: "He's a right gobshite, always spouting rubbish!" The term likely originated from the Irish word "gob," which means mouth, combined with the English word "shite" to create a colorful insult.

Acting the maggot - (AK-ting the MAG-it) A term used to describe someone who is behaving foolishly or mischievously. It's a common phrase in Ireland, particularly when referring to someone who is being annoying or causing trouble. Example: "Will you stop acting the maggot and focus on your work?" The term likely originated from the wriggling, aimless movement of maggots.

The craic was ninety - (the crack was nine-tee) A phrase used to describe a situation or event that was particularly enjoyable or fun. It's a popular phrase in Ireland, especially among older generations. Example: "Last night's party was great, the craic was ninety!" The term "craic" comes from the Irish language and means fun or good times.

Pissed as a newt - A term used to describe someone who is very drunk. Example: "He was out all night and he's as pissed as a newt." The origins of the phrase are uncertain, but it may come from the belief that newts have a similar reaction to alcohol as humans do.

I'M AS PISSED AS A NEWT!!!

Holy Joe - A term used to describe someone who is overly religious or sanctimonious. Example: "She's such a Holy Joe, always preaching about morality." The origin of the term is unclear, but it may come from the name Joseph, which is associated with religious piety.

Thick as two short planks - A term used to describe someone who is very stupid. Example: "He can't figure it out, he's as thick as two short planks." The phrase likely originated from the idea that two short planks placed side by side would be too thin to support anything.

Manky - (MAN-kee) A term used to describe something that is dirty or unpleasant. It's commonly used in Ireland, particularly when referring to unwashed items or unhygienic situations. Example: "I can't eat off those plates, they're manky." The word likely comes from the Irish word "manach," meaning dirty or filthy.

Laughing, Crying, and Everything in Between: The Emotional Range of Traditional Irish Storytelling

"Irish people are the world's best storytellers, and their slang is like poetry."

Chris O'Dowd

Oh, the joys of storytelling. It's a time-honored tradition in Irish culture, and believe me, we have some of the best storytellers in the world. The Irish know how to spin a good yarn, from the famous seancha (storytellers) of old Ireland to modern-day writers and poets.

But what qualities distinguish a good storyteller? There is no magic formula, but a few pints of Guinness can't hurt. I'm joking (sort of). In all seriousness, storytelling is all about capturing the attention of the audience and transporting them on a journey. It's about transporting them to another time and place with your words, making them feel like they're a part of the story.

The great Seán Faoláin was one of the most famous Irish storytellers of all time. He was a master of the short story and wrote some of modern Irish literature's most iconic tales. His stories were full of wit, humor, and insight into the human condition.

A good storyteller, however, does not have to be a literary genius. Indeed, some of the best stories are those that are told from the heart. Whether it's a story about your own personal triumphs and struggles or a funny childhood anecdote, the key is to make the story relatable and engaging.

So, how do you go about becoming a good storyteller? It all begins with practice. Begin by telling stories to your friends and family, and don't be afraid to try out new styles and techniques. You might discover that you have an undiscovered talent for storytelling.

Another suggestion is to research the greats. Try to figure out what makes Seán Faoláin's, James Joyce's, or any other great Irish storyteller's stories so compelling. Is it because of the language? What about the pacing? What about the characters? Apply what you've learned to your own storytelling style.

Ultimately, storytelling is about bringing people together and making connections. It is about sharing our experiences and emotions in a way that others can relate to. So, whether you're a natural storyteller or just getting started, remember to have fun and appreciate the power of the spoken word. Sláinte!

Chapter Nineteen

"Putting the Cork in the Bottle"

CONCLUSION

"When the Irish language dies out, the English language will be left with a great void to fill... and it will have to fill it with some other beautiful, expressive, and rich language... like Irish slang!"

Colm Toibin, Irish author

And so, we come to the end of our journey through the world of Irish slang. We've explored the many facets of Irish life, from the music to the sports, the food to the festivals, and everything in between. We've laughed at the irreverent wit of the Irish, marveled at their linguistic acrobatics, and learned a thing or two about their unique way of seeing the world.

But our journey doesn't have to end here. If there's one thing we've learned about the Irish, it's that they love to talk, and there's always more to learn. So, the next time you find yourself in a cozy pub or chatting with a friendly local, don't be afraid to ask about their favorite slang terms or expressions. Who knows what colorful stories and insights you might uncover?

As we close the book on this adventure, let's raise a glass to the Irish and their way with words. May their humor, creativity, and irreverence continue to inspire us all. Sláinte!

A quick note about the contents of this book:

Every effort has been made to ensure that the slang phrases, words, and expressions mentioned in this book are as accurate and up to date as possible. Of course, I could have written a dictionary of Irish slang that's longer than the River Shannon, but then you'd be reading until Saint Patrick's Day next year. Instead, what this book provides is a simple guide to how the Irish actually speak today. We tried our best to avoid the "craic" clichés (oops, we said it again...)

Instead, our aim was to show you the real, everyday language of the Irish people, whether you're in Dublin or Dingle.

But most importantly, we hope you've had a good laugh at some of the mad expressions and witty words of the Emerald Isle. We've certainly had great craic writing it! And a special thanks to the fantastic illustrator, Sam Davies, whose artwork has brought this book to life.

If you've enjoyed this book, we'd be ever so grateful if you could leave us a review on Amazon. Your feedback and support mean the world to us. And if you've spotted a mistake or want to suggest something for the next edition, feel free to reach out to us using the email address below:

jeffwatson688@gmail.com

Chapter Twenty

A NIFTY LITTLE GLOSSARY OF IRISH SLANG TERMS

"Irish slang is a bit like a secret code. Once you know it, you feel like you're part of the club."

Saoirse Ronan

As we reach the end of our journey through the colorful and quirky world of Irish slang, let's take a moment to appreciate one of the many gems we've encountered: the word "**nifty**". This delightful term encapsulates the essence of Irish ingenuity and resourcefulness, referring to a clever trick, gadget, or skill that makes life just a little bit easier. Whether it's a nifty travel case for your headphones or a nifty trick to open a beer with a lighter, the Irish have a knack for finding simple yet effective solutions to life's little problems.

But what do you do when you can't quite recall the meaning of a particular slang term? Fear not, dear reader, for I have compiled a comprehensive list of every single term and expression mentioned in this book. So, the next time you find yourself scratching your head over the meaning of a particular phrase, simply consult this handy guide and jog your memory.

I hope this journey through the wild and wonderful world of Irish slang has been as entertaining and enlightening for you as it has been for me. From the bawdy to the brilliant, the irreverent to the ingenious, Irish slang is a testament to the wit, creativity, and irrepressible spirit of the Irish people.

Sláinte!

Made in the USA
Monee, IL
05 April 2023